Women Who Dared

D0509367

Library of Congress
A Book of Postcards

Pomegranate Artbooks
San Francisco

Pomegranate Artbooks
Box 6099
Rohnert Park, CA 94927

ISBN 1-56640-250-6
Pomegranate Catalog No. A657

Pomegranate publishes books of postcards on a wide range of subjects.
Please write to the publisher for more information

Cover design by Mark Koenig
Printed in Korea

"Considering the length of time that women have been dependent, is it surprising that some of them hug their chains, and fawn like the spaniel?"—Mary Wollstonecraft, 1792

In this *Women Who Dared*, the second volume of this title published by Pomegranate Artbooks, we present thirty women who decidedly did not fawn and hug their chains. Each in some way exemplifies the power to be found in challenging circumstance and limitation, in breaking through adversity, doubt, loneliness and ridicule. Their struggles and victories are richly chronicled in the collections of the Library of Congress, from which the material here is drawn.

The people and accomplishments depicted herein represent a proud response to the gauntlet thrown down by Susan B. Anthony in 1863:

"Forget conventionalisms; forget what the world will say, whether you are in your place or out of your place; think your best thoughts, speak your best words, do your best works, looking [only] to your own conscience for approval."

WOMEN WHO DARED

Josephine Baker (American, 1906–1975) danced in
vaudeville houses and joined a traveling dance troupe
when she was sixteen. In 1923 she landed a chorus line
spot in a Broadway show, but it was in Paris two years
later that she stepped fully into the spotlight in *La
Revue Negre*. She was irreverent and exotic, known for
her magnetic stage presence and outrageous promo-
tional antics. A politically courageous woman, Baker
spoke and acted against racism throughout her life and
was a member of the French Resistance in World War
II, for which she was awarded the Legion of Honor.

Pomegranate, Box 6099, Rohnert Park, CA 94927

WOMEN WHO DARED

Margaret Mead (American, 1901–1978) focused her considerable energies on the developing science of anthropology. She traveled the world, living within, studying and comparing a variety of cultures, and writing about them in over thirty books. The vivid, straightforward writing style she revealed in the first of these, *Coming of Age in Samoa* (1928)—still the best-selling anthropology volume of all time—helped create a reputation and fame that followed her throughout her life.

Pomegranate, Box 6099, Rohnert Park, CA 94927

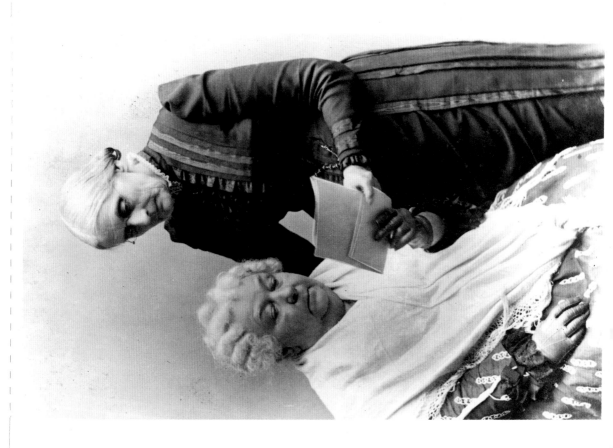

Women Who Dared

Elizabeth Cady Stanton (American, 1815–1902) is best known as the lifelong political compatriot of Susan B. Anthony and principal author of the famous 1848 Declaration of Sentiments ("we hold these truths to be self-evident, that all men and women are created equal. . . ."). Stanton's extraordinary vitality, passion and intellectual force made her a pillar of the women's rights movement for more than fifty years, and her majesty of expression speaks no less inspiringly to readers of today.

Pomegranate, Box 6099, Rohnert Park, CA 94927

WOMEN WHO DARED

Pearl Buck (American, 1892–1973) was the first American woman to win the Nobel Prize in literature (1938). She spent most of her early life in China, where her parents, and later both she and her first husband, were missionaries. She became widely recognized with the publication of *The Good Earth* in 1931; in 1932, after a heated public controversy with the Presbyterian Board of Missions, Buck resigned as a missionary. She moved back to the U.S. and continued to write novels and other materials devoted to increasing understanding between all peoples.

Pomegranate, Box 6099, Rohnert Park, CA 94927

WOMEN WHO DARED

Georgia O'Keeffe (American, 1887–1986) wanted to be
a painter from the time she was twelve. By the time of
her death at age ninety-nine, she had left a more
profound mark on American art than perhaps any other
woman save Mary Cassatt, with a style that was
uncategorizable yet instantly recognizable as her own.
The story of her life is as well known as her work,
especially her artistic and personal alliance with
pioneering art photographer Alfred Stieglitz.

Pomegranate, Box 6099, Rohnert Park, CA 94927

WOMEN WHO DARED

Gabrielle Chanel (French, 1883?–1971) opened her first boutique (Deauville, France) in 1913, when women had still not shaken the external vestiges of nineteenth-century restriction: the corsets, petticoats and impossibly ruffly getups of the day's fashion. Chanel, who had been making her own clothes for several years, virtually invented the concept of sportswear and developed a vision of uncomplicated female dress, the impact of which was probably unequaled by any other single designer of the twentieth century. She built a fashion empire on providing women with comfortable clothes, as well as her No. 5 perfume.

Pomegranate, Box 6099, Rohnert Park, CA 94927

WOMEN WHO DARED

Carrie Chapman Catt (American, 1859–1947) was Susan B. Anthony's hand-picked successor to lead the national suffrage movement. Catt developed a comprehensive plan for achieving national woman suffrage via constitutional amendment, and her relentless attention to every aspect of its execution in the Congress and the states was widely credited in the 1920 victory. Having foreseen the victory, Catt also had begun laying the groundwork a year earlier for the educational organization established as the League of Women Voters.

Pomegranate, Box 6099, Rohnert Park, CA 94927

WOMEN WHO DARED

Althea Gibson (American, b. 1927) became the player who broke the racial barrier in championship tennis. She was a star in the Negro youth leagues in New York by 1943, and five years later she won the women's title for the first of five times. In 1950 she became the first African American to play at the U.S. Open and, in 1951, at Wimbledon. Beginning in 1956 she burned up the tournament circuit for three years, sweeping most of the majors (including the 1957 Wimbledon, from which this photo is taken) in both 1957 and 1958. Gibson was elected to the National Lawn Tennis Hall of Fame in 1971.

Pomegranate, Box 6099, Rohnert Park, CA 94927

WOMEN WHO DARED

Sacajawea (Shoshone, c. 1786–1812) grew in prominence in the romance of the frontier to be (erroneously) called the chief guide to Lewis and Clark. But her accomplishments are real enough: she accompanied the Lewis and Clark expedition, for which her husband was interpreter and guide, and she enabled the explorers to communicate with many of the tribes they encountered. She led the way through the Bozeman Pass and during at least one critical point in the expedition intervened to obtain much-needed horses from the Shoshone, her own tribe.

Pomegranate, Box 6099, Rohnert Park, CA 94927

WOMEN WHO DARED

Dame Ethel Smyth's (English, 1858–1944) two best works, the *Mass in D* and an opera, *The Wreckers*, have gained enduring critical admiration. She is remembered as a composer who overcame all manner of obstacles and prejudice to make a lasting mark, a militant suffragist who conducted her "March of the Women" from a jail cell with her toothbrush, and a literary raconteur of high style.

Pomegranate, Box 6099, Rohnert Park, CA 94927

WOMEN WHO DARED

Milena Jesenka (Czech, 1896–1944), the recipient of writer Franz Kafka's most passionate letters, was a talented and politically committed journalist who took a stand early on against the rise of National Socialism in Germany. She was arrested in 1939 by the Nazis and sent to the concentration camp at Ravensbruck, where she became a symbol of the unbowed and unbroken spirit that none can imprison. She died in the camp less than a month before D day, but her close friend and sister prisoner Margarete Buber-Neumann told the story of their experience in her haunting book *Milena* (1977).

Pomegranate, Box 6099, Rohnert Park, CA 94927

WOMEN WHO DARED

Sappho (Greek, c. 615–? B.C.) was among the first poets to turn the epic quest inward to the personal, subjective self and is the only female lyricist of antiquity whose work has come down to our age. She lived most of her life on the Greek isle of Lesbos and is thus regarded as the archetypal Lesbian, especially for the coterie of young women with whom she surrounded herself and of whom she wrote with open eroticism.

Pomegranate, Box 6099, Rohnert Park, CA 94927

Nineteenth-century engraving
General Collections
© Library of Congress

WOMEN WHO DARED

Mae West (American, 1893–1980) had her first big success in 1926 with the play *Sex*, which she wrote, produced and starred in—and which ultimately was closed down by the local vice squad. Her signature persona, the hilariously overwrought, offhand femme fatale, made a complex statement of sexual politics and perception. Yet as an entertainer first and foremost, West took seriously her obligation to amuse, and she fulfilled it so well that at the height of her career in the early 1930s she was the highest-paid woman in Hollywood.

Pomegranate, Box 6099, Rohnert Park, CA 94927

WOMEN WHO DARED

Ida Wells-Barnett (American, 1862–1931) fought all her life against racial injustice, but is today honored most for her relentless campaign against racial lynching. She was an early predecessor of Rosa Parks in her refusal, in May 1884, to give up a train seat in the white section. Removed by force, she sued and won in the circuit court, but the Tennessee Supreme Court later reversed the decision. She became a full-time journalist in 1891, and for many years she defied mob violence and terror to train a relentless and harsh light on the national disgrace of lynching.

Pomegranate, Box 6099, Rohnert Park, CA 94927

WOMEN WHO DARED

Katherine Stinson (American, 1891–1977) earned her pilot's license in 1912, when aviation was still considered the province of daredevils if not maniacs. She proceeded to make her mark not only as one of the gutsiest stunt flyers of her generation, but as a pioneer who contributed much to the furthering of aviation-mindedness throughout the world.

Pomegranate, Box 6099, Rohnert Park, CA 94927

WOMEN WHO DARED

Helen Hunt Jackson (American, 1830–1885) is best known for her 1881 book *A Century of Dishonor*, an unflinching account of the greed, arrogance and bad faith that characterized the history of U.S. government treatment of Native Americans. A tireless fact-finder and agitator, Jackson circulated pamphlets and petitions, wrote to newspapers, prodded and hounded officials and even challenged Theodore Roosevelt to a dialogue about the plight of the Indians in America.

Pomegranate, Box 6099, Rohnert Park, CA 94927

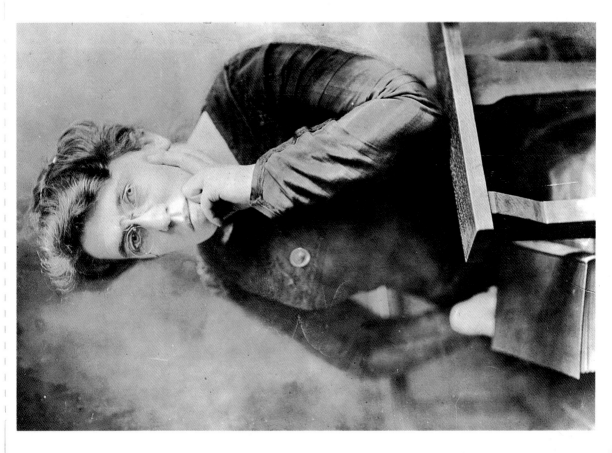

WOMEN WHO DARED

Emma Goldman (Russian, 1869–1940) is remembered as one of the most uncompromising and courageous radicals of her age, who agitated on behalf of "liberty unrestricted by man-made law." She fled to the United States as a teenager, where she was radicalized by the conditions of the urban laboring masses and the prevailing socialist and anarchist currents. For her continuous activism she was jailed many times, gained national notoriety by the 1890s and eventually was deported from the U.S.

Pomegranate, Box 6099, Rohnert Park, CA 94927

WOMEN WHO DARED

Lois Weber (American, 1881–1939) was one of the first women to make a significant mark as an independent filmmaker and was also one of the very first filmmakers to use the medium as a means of speaking out on social issues. She wrote, acted, directed, designed sets and costumes, edited and developed negatives. She also was involved in sound experimentation for films. In 1917 she established her own production house, and its films were released through Universal Pictures for the rest of her career.

Pomegranate, Box 6099, Rohnert Park, CA 94927

Women Who Dared

Gertrude Bell (English, 1868–1926) was among the first women in England to gain access to higher education. She became attracted to the Middle East when she visited relatives in Teheran, and eventually she traveled all over the region, often alone, chronicling journeys and excavations in many areas where she was the first European woman to ever have been seen. In 1915 Bell was tapped by the British government for the first of several diplomatic posts, which took her first to Basra and then to Baghdad. She became an influential diplomat and political analyst.

Pomegranate, Box 6099, Rohnert Park, CA 94927

WOMEN WHO DARED

Sarah Bernhardt (French, 1886–1939) was arguably the most commanding personality in the history of modern Western theater. She was an actor who had the rare quality of at once defining and embodying her times. "The Divine Sarah" discovered acting in early adolescence and went on to innumerable triumphs, opening her own theater and touring internationally.

Pomegranate, Box 6099, Rohnert Park, CA 94927

WOMEN WHO DARED

Maria Mitchell (American, 1818–1889) was the first person to find a comet by telescope, in 1847. Her achievement brought her international recognition and marked the beginning of an illustrious career. She was the first woman to be elected to both the American Academy of Arts and Sciences and the American Association for the Advancement of Science. In 1865 she took the post of director of the observatory at Vassar College, where she taught and conducted research for twenty years.

Pomegranate, Box 6099, Rohnert Park, CA 94927

WOMEN WHO DARED

Bessie Smith (American, 1894–1937) made her first recording in 1923 ("Downhearted Blues"), and it quickly established her as the most successful black recording artist of her day. Her personal and musical power as a blues and jazz singer pushed out the boundaries of both female and African-American expression for a new mass audience.

Pomegranate, Box 6099, Rohnert Park, CA 94927

WOMEN WHO DARED

Mourning Dove (Okanogan, c. 1882–1936), an Okanogan Indian of the Northwest coast, was sent to a mission school as a child. She put her mission education to use in the service of her native culture by becoming a writer. She became an important chronicler of the lifeways of her people, thus preserving a great deal of knowledge that otherwise might have been lost. Her best-known book, *Coyote Stories*, first published in 1933 and still in print today, is one of the first collections of native stories that was gathered and transcribed by a Native American.

Pomegranate, Box 6099, Rohnert Park, CA 94927

WOMEN WHO DARED

Lucretia Mott (American, 1793–1880) organized, with
Elizabeth Cady Stanton, the famous Seneca Falls con-
vention of 1848, in which American women made their
first public demand for equal rights under the law.
Mott's influence upon many first-generation suffragists
was profound. She was a tireless, lifelong activist and
eloquent speaker whose "feminine" demeanor served
well to refute those who tried to ridicule suffragists as
hysterical, ungodly and imitation-men.

Pomegranate, Box 6099, Rohnert Park, CA 94927

WOMEN WHO DARED

Edith Sampson (American, 1901–1979), a pioneering African American, female law student and then lawyer, racked up many firsts in her career and came to be widely known and respected as a practicing attorney in Chicago. In 1962 she became the first black woman judge in America, and she later served as an alternate delegate to the United Nations, traveling widely abroad as a goodwill ambassador.

Pomegranate, Box 6099, Rohnert Park, CA 94927

WOMEN WHO DARED

Gabriela Mistral (Chilean, 1889–1957) is known in Chile as "the spiritual queen of Latin America." A poet and educator, she was an activist on behalf of homeless children, reorganized the library and rural school systems of Mexico, and became the first Latin American writer to be awarded the Nobel Prize in literature, in 1945.

Pomegranate, Box 6099, Rohnert Park, CA 94927

Women Who Dared

Margaret Sanger (American, 1883–1966) was a nurse who took it upon herself to find practical methods of birth control (her coinage) that could be made available to any woman. She found herself at odds with government and organized religion, both of which would battle her furiously for years as she sought to make birth control a fundamental human right. That American women possess this right today is due in great measure to her valiant and incessant efforts.

Pomegranate, Box 6099, Rohnert Park, CA 94927

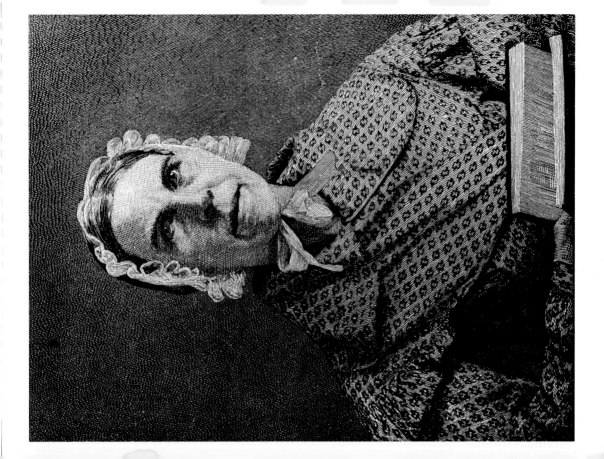

WOMEN WHO DARED

Sarah M. Grimké (American, 1792–1873) and her sister Angelina became the first women to speak in public against slavery and then for women's rights. Enduring immense public vilification in their native Charleston, South Carolina, they were among the most prominent and effective activists of their day in both arenas.

Pomegranate, Box 6099, Rohnert Park, CA 94927

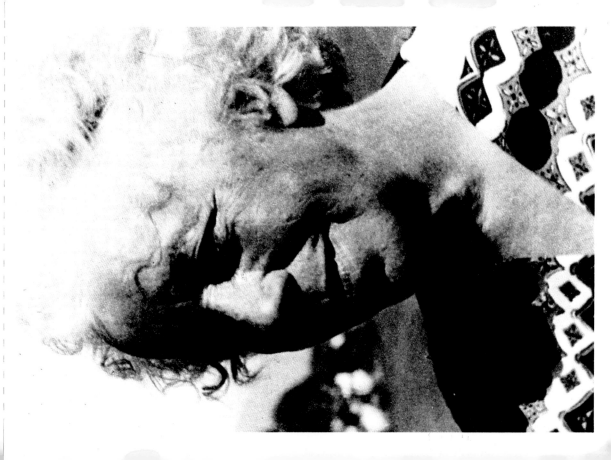

WOMEN WHO DARED

Karen Horney (German, 1885–1952) was a giant of twentieth-century psychoanalytic theory and practice. She liberated Freudian theory not only from its more pronounced androcentric blinders but from the cult of sterile dogmatism that had come to envelop it by the 1920s. Her theories of feminine psychology sought to extend Freud's work to encompass female reality as well as dynamic factors of culture and environment.

Pomegranate, Box 6099, Rohnert Park, CA 94927

WOMEN WHO DARED

Amelia Bloomer (American, 1818–1894) began publishing the *Lily*, a women's newspaper that was probably the first to be edited entirely by a woman, in 1849. The *Lily* concerned itself primarily with temperance, suffrage and women's rights, including dress reform. Bloomer became a defender of the "Turkish trouser" costume, full-cut pantaloons worn under a short skirt, and her name was forever linked to the garment.

Pomegranate, Box 6099, Rohnert Park, CA 94927